# RED WAVE

## TASK FORCE 2020

*Handbook for a Grassroots Movement
of Proactive Voters.*

# JOSEPH DILEONARDO

outskirts
press

# DEDICATION

*To my Wife Sharon for all she does ; my Daughter Christina for her joy and determination to make a difference in the world; and our Grandson Harrison who is the future for America and the world.*

# Table of Contents

# PREFACE

My last book was also non-fiction, entitled: *VIETNAM WAR: DEFINING MOMENT FOR AMERICA, Remembrances and Reflections of an Army Intelligence Officer.* 2013, Outskirts Press, Parker, Colorado. which is still in print and available at all book outlets. Reading that book might help you understand why I wrote this current book.

My first foray into politics came early. I ran for vice-president of my middle school and my older brother Anthony ran for president. We were both elected at the Edwina Benner School, Sunnyvale, California. That was the start of a long and continuous relationship with all things political.

In high school, I developed a love and interest in American history. In my senior year, I read two books which had a lifelong impact on my views of America and its societal direction. The first book was *Brave New World* by author Aldous Huxley which predicted the rise of the socialist "nanny state" of Europe and America. The second book was *1984* by George Orwell which predicted the rise of sweeping mind control and authoritarian societies.

In college, I majored in political science and was elected President of the Democrat club at University of Santa Clara. I became disenchanted with the party when our club supported the Civil Rights Act of 1964 but the Democrats in Congress did not. I was later elected to Gardner Neighborhood Center, part of the War on Poverty commenced by President Lyndon Johnson. After one year, found there was no real "war" to end poverty but rather a program to build a new administrative empire and organize communities for political purposes. This is a scenario played repeatedly by the Democrat Party since those days.

I attended law school and was given extension for active duty by the army as a commissioned reserve officer. During law school, I began to question the leadership of the Democrat party. I was not a fan of a war that was in "limbo." After graduation, I went on active duty, and yes, served over 13 months in Vietnam as an intelligence officer. My loyalty to the Democrat Party was eroding. It was not just that they had made a mess of the war, but something else. Something which began with an "anti-war movement" but became little disguised as a commencement of the culture war. The Democrat Party sold its soul to the leftist progressives behind the movement and legitimized their causes.

I followed through with attempting political activity. I did run for county supervisor in 1974. I lost, but did get appointed to the first consumers affairs commission of Santa Clara County, California in 1975.

I moved to Colorado in 2009 and became active in politics again. I was elected Precinct Committeeman, member of the Elbert County Republican Committee, elected a county convention and state convention delegate. We lost elections we should have won. I also, could see, as a society, we were moving more and more to the left, more to the politically correct "nanny state."

I spent some time reflecting on my life and the society and culture now embracing America. I then wrote and published a book in 2013. At page105, I wrote the following: "Vietnam War was a catalyst for the start of a culture counterculture war still being waged today with, the stakes-the very Soul of America." I was not the only one who could see and predict the ensuing culture war. But few acknowledged or took the counterculture seriously.

Then in 2016, a disruptor-an outsider, threw his hat in the ring and ran for President, as the Republican nominee. When he spoke, he did not shy away from the real gut issue for America. Did we want to make America Great Again, or did we want to embrace the slippery slope of socialism and endless "political correctness authoritarianism?" America chose MAGA and Trump became our 45<sup>th</sup> President.

However, the left and the Democrats became hysterical with the results of the 2016 election, which returned all control of the House of Representatives. the Senate and the Presidency to the Republicans. The Democrats went into attack mode and made it clear, the war for the "hearts and minds of America" is not over yet. The Democrats were able to take the majority of the House of Representatives in the 2018 election. This knocked some of the complacency from Republicans.

I decided to write this book. It is meant to be a handbook for the proactive voters who support the Red Wave of conservatives, MAGA supporters and those who generally support the ideals of the "greatest generation." The midterm elections made it also clear the Democrats and progressives are ready to do battle and have been emboldened by their victory in the House of Representatives. Come join me in a new grass roots movement that I have named the "Red Wave Task Force Target 2020."

# INTRODUCTION

America has been at war, a civil war since the mid 1960's. That war has been for the very soul of our country. It has been a culture versus counterculture war fought insidiously at all levels. You may have not known of this but after many years and in retrospect you have seen its effects on society today. The war has often been one-sided. There has been a constant attack by the progressives and the "left" on many of the longstanding institutions in America. We have seen some of the most beloved traditions and institutions mocked and ridiculed until as Huxley would say, they were made into dirty words-like "marriage", "family" "patriotism" "love of country" and so many more.

Elections are the most productive and humane way to change power, control and policies in a nation. For nearly all of mankind, war and violence has been the only way to transfer power. However, even though we do not shed blood and destroy property, an election is a war none the less. The outcome and importance in affecting millions of lives makes it just as serious as any shooting war. And, to win a war it takes plans, strategy, tactics and true patriots. Our intent here is to provide suggestions, recommendations, mentoring and guides to form a grass-roots movement to win that war in November 2020.

We start by giving you a blueprint for victory and then spell out a specific strategy to win. The rest of the book is full of concrete easy to understand tactics and actions to conduct the campaign and win. This a handbook and a workbook. There are personal worksheets and self-surveys at the back of the book to assist you, but the true inspiration and motivation can only come from dccp inside you.

**CHAPTER 1**

# MAKING OF A "GRASSROOTS MOVEMENT"

Historians have chronicled many grassroots movements in America, especially those related to political movements. However, in modern times political strategists have used "grassroots movement" as a buzz word for something they hoped to create with expensive ads and paid campaign workers. True movements are from the people, not expensive ads and professional campaigns.

The first great grassroots movement was the American revolution. It is that movement we will compare and give organization to the current movement generally known as the Red Wave and Make America Great movement. We will refer to much of the campaign with the same military type terminology that campaigns in America do to this day, such as "War rooms" "Strategy and tactics," and "attack ads" and more.

We are not attempting to form a new organization or institution. We are trying to provide people with the tools and practical knowledge to really effect a victory in the elections of 2020. The grass roots movement is to provide a pool of people who want a Red Wave victory in November 2020. These grassroots taskforce patriots who can fill the ranks of the campaign in a way that each person decides.

We have provided a three-tier identification of participation, that should be useful in making your decision

**THE CITIZEN SOLDIER**

"It proves more forcibly the necessity of obliging every citizen to be a soldier; this was the case with the Greeks and Romans and must be that of every free state." Thomas Jefferson, June 19, 1813. The citizen soldier has been a part of America since the Revolutionary War. We have extended the concept AND THE DUTY to the political conflicts as well.

A few years back the United States Army, ran a massive advertisement campaign for recruitment. The branding was "The Army of One." They made the point that an army is only as good as each and every soldier. Also, the Red Wave Task Force is only as good as the individual voter.

We do not expect much of the person. First, we ask you do a personal inventory. (a worksheet in Appendix A) You need to find out all the elected positions that you will be voting on in the primary and general elections. Use the inventory as a way of helping you keep informed on the campaigns as they develop.

Second, we would like you to follow a very simple protocol we have devised that does not take you out of your comfort zone. We do believe that if every person who reads this book does one thing, follow this protocol, there should be a landside Red Wave victory in 2020.

***The Five Step Protocol***
1. Register to vote and see that you family does as well for the primary election;
2. Vote in the primary election;
3. Make sure you and family are registered for the general election;
4. Vote in the general election;
5. Ask just one other person to complete this protocol for themselves.

This is simple and can be very effective. It also does not preclude you from taking other simple actions that would add to the overall effort to win the elections in November 2020. That would include going to a campaign headquarter and obtaining a house sign, a bumper sticker and as many flyers and brochures you could reasonably handout. You might consider sending a small donation to some of the candidates as they do need funds to hire accountant or attorney to assist in meeting the filing requirements imposed on the candidates who accept donations for their campaigns.

You might even find these simple actions have caused you to start a more determined interest in the campaigns and consider becoming even more active. Whether you do or don't, you should continue reading so you fully understand how the Red Wave Task Force will work

## THE MINUTEMAN

"The Battles of Lexington and Concord," took place April 19, 1775. The American colonists in 1774 formed a provisional colonial government and set up their own type militia calling themselves minutemen. By 1775 the King had become angered by what he saw as rebellious behavior by a group of British subjects. An order had gone out to British troops in Boston to go to Lexington and Concord and seize the arms and ammunition of the "militia." There were at least three open skirmishes with the colonialist suffering the most casualties. However, word had gone out to the Minutemen and they arrived in larger numbers. The tide had turned and the British forces returned to Boston without the seized weapons, and were harassed and suffered casualties on the way. Without the swift reinforcements (the first "flash mob" of its time), there might never have been a United States of America.

Proudly, you can be the modern Minuteman for the Red Wave Task Force. If you cannot devote much time and effort to the movement, but still want to do as much as possible, then you are perfect for this. You help when called on and when you find you have time to do extra projects for the movement. Here is our vision of these modern Minutemen.

You would do all that was set out previously for the Citizen soldier. Register, vote and get someone else to do the same thing. You should also get some bumper stickers and lawn signs. Next fill out Appendix A and B and have the handbook with you always as a place to refer and make notes. A spiral notebook would help as you could write down contacts and important notes. You do not need a lot of material do be a good minuteman, you need desire and a few aids. From the two appendix you will need to find your initial candidate and party contacts that need your help. We will try and assist by setting up a website to pass along opportunities for you and requests from campaigns needing Minutemen.

Under tactics and plans chapters we will discuss various activities just suited for Minutemen. But do not be limited by just our suggestions, let your imagination be your guide as well. We cannot however stress enough that a campaign requires good networking and communication. Fill your notebook with contacts and stay in contact through November 3, 2020.

## THE PATRIOT

We need a number of "Patriots" to step up and give of their "time" and "talent" to assist in the success of the Red Wave Taskforce. Sacrifice has always been required to succeed as a Patriot. This group is made up of people who have the time and talent to do more than others. We will try and provide some ideas and recommendations for you to do just that- make a difference. The decision is of course up to you as to how and where you serve.

### *Become a Candidate*

You are the most committed and often a true self-starter. Its from your ranks the most important job- consideration of being a candidate should come. This is not something we ask of everyone nor do we take this lightly. If you have considered running for office, please take the time to reflect.

An elected official is a very serious and somber position. The number one trait that this author can give is be humble but not afraid. Anyone who has had to master serious decisions about persons lives knows the awful dread that can come from fear of being wrong and harming another human. It is something that comes with the position. Let it be the humble not arrogant and with the highest intentions.

If you consider running for office, we address the subject more in the Chapter "The Model Campaign Organization."

### *Volunteer to Be an Election Official.*

You have to become non-partisan for these very important positions. The voters have seen so many news reports of mistakes, glitches, and sometimes out and out fraud at the polling places and in the counting and handling of votes. An election must be credible as it must be fair and accurate. Not a lot of glory, but very necessary. No game such as football, baseball and others could be satisfactory without referees. No Court case could be completed without an impartial judge to provide a fair trial and insist on proper procedures.

If this interests you, contact the head election official in your county and ask how you can volunteer to be a poll person or some other position of working in the elections. Most Counties provide some compensation for your time, but it is usually not much and certainly not the major reason for taking on this assignment. Most of you have remembrances of undecided elections and voter recounts and all the missteps and mistakes that caused these events. Be part of the solution and volunteer.

### *Volunteer for the Republican Party*

We have heard many complain that the Republican Party picks the candidates and directs us to vote for them. If you are a Republican, you are the party. You can affect a lot of what your party does at every level by being active and proactive as a party member. The Party is organized differently in almost every state but usually has Party groups at the County and State level. You need to find out where the party headquarters are. The best place to start is to look up the Republican Party for you state and review their website. They have contact information and you can inform them of what it is you wish to do. They can assist you. When election time rolls around they need an army of poll watchers and observers during the ballot tallies. Yes, it might be a bit boring, but it is necessary. If we do not have enough Republican volunteers, there will be unobserved tallies observed only by Democrats.

If you join the Party, in many states that makes you eligible to be a delegate to state and national conventions. Each state has different rules and procedures for being involved in Party politics. If you are a proactive voter this could be your special mission for election 2020. Contact the Party's state office and ask how you can become a precinct captain, a delegate to state and national convention. Find out how those people you see on television casting votes were chosen to go to the national convention. Find out how you can be one of the delegates who sits in the platform committee or the rules committee.

As with all matters discussed in this handbook, we will try and provide additional and updated matter in our website in the coming months.

### *Intelligence / Counter Intelligence / Analysts*

We speak about this mission in describing the model campaign organization. The Taskforce needs persons individually or in small groups to take on the part of modern day campaigns that have become critical to an election. The mission consists of three parts;

1. Intelligence gathering about opponents, their issues and campaigns,
2. Analyze all data retrieved and prepare an intelligence report: which would
3. include a rendition of the data you found and your conclusions as an analyst.

Counter-intelligence is the gathering information on the plans and activities of your opponents directed at Red Wave candidates.

In these modern tech times, the best intelligence and counterintelligence persons are very into IT and research through multiple sources. It is best to work in groups. There are many of you already doing this function, and we talk about that when we discuss the Internet Warriors. Also, it is important for an intelligence person be designated for each campaign and we speak about that when discussing the Model Campaign Office

The most important intelligence report you will make is a dossier. A Dossier is a detailed report on as person or a subject (Note Author was trained as a counter- intelligence officer by the US Army with specific training in background investigation). Most by now have read or heard something about the dossier prepared by a private security company Fusion GPS and the report by former British MI6 agent Christopher Steele. If you know about that dossier then you know how bad it was. It is mainly mentioned here because it is an example OF WHAT YOU SHOULD NOT DO IN PREPARING A DOSSIER. In political circles they call the dossier an opposition research report. Whatever you call it, you must be absolutely meticulous in your research and in how you write your report.

In recent times we have found that some critical, possibly damaging background information, has been overlooked. One area is high school and college yearbooks. Many of those yearbooks contain written messages or pictures that could now be construed as racist or bigoted or show callousness towards women. We have even seen in the campaign for Roy Moore, the opposition use some suspicious added ink colored writing to portray Moore as having known some teenage girl. Make sure you check all sources and do not exclude high school days.

Verify your investigation with multiple sources. Use the Freedom of Information Act to obtain copies from ANY government agency to get documentation for your search or verification. The Act is known as FOIA and it has been the single greatest weapon the citizens have in forcing the government to be transparent. Every state has a FOIA as does the United States government. These Acts are often updated and modified, so research your own state. The agencies however are charged with assisting you in using FOIA. Do not hesitate to follow up a report of an arrest by seeking a copy of the police report. The reports might come with redacted parts. The FOIA request alone is more to let government know you are watching. Sometimes a mass request for certain documents, like the emails of Hilary Clinton, would send a message that the public takes the matter seriously.

Groups like Judicial Watch will file suits in court to demand the reports and unredacted reports. Check with watch dog groups to see if they have already sought the same documents you are seeking. Develop a working relationship with the various sources for information. The key is not just getting the data but rather what you do with it.

Data and documents and other factual material ARE NOT INTELLIGENCE. To reach the status as "intelligence," the data and sources must be analyzed and an intelligence officer must draw conclusions by "connecting the dots." Intelligence analysis is a skill, a science, and an art. There really are not many people who qualify as intelligence analysts.

Intelligence is of no value if it is not published or transmitted to someone in the need to know. It does no good for you to discover that a report by a news agency is bogus, unless you can send your rebuttal to the same or larger audience. Source your intelligence. If you know it would be of special use to a candidate or a group, contact them and send them the material. If it is used to rebut or neutralize fake or bogus news or reports, then wide spread distribution of your intelligence is required. Like every other member of the Taskforce, a communication system and protocol of your own should be in place. We talk about this in our chapter on tactics and plans.

### *Event Coordinator*

The picture at the back of the book is of the Author in uniform with his horse at a sacred ceremony: Memorial Day. Monday May 25, 2020 is Memorial Day during election year. Every candidate needs to attend a memorial service. Not because it is a great photo-op, but because it will renew the feeling of duty, honor and sacrifice for this Country. You will see the graves of men and women who gave all so you could run for elected office in a free country. You need to make them proud.

Every campaign has need of someone who is an event coordinator. That person insures that no special day or event passes without their candidate participating in some way. If you have the ability of arranging and organizing events, then volunteer.

The events can be simple as a "wave and honk" street corner affair you can arrange, meet the candidate coffee get together, or a simple barbeque at your home. You invite and candidates will come to your home. Or, you can respond and invite others as well to an event that has already been organized.

One tactic that we intend to use is a political equivalent of the "flash mob." It's called the "cloudcrowd." Using the internet network, "telephone trees" and online bulletin boards online, notice goes out to crowd meet at a political event. It's a way the "flash mob" rallies and events with maximum turnout and often overflow. It shows "mass" and "momentum."

### Internet Warriors

January 19, 2019, an incident occurred in Washington, D.C. Most of America became aware of the incident, shortly after it occurred, as a short video was played on social network and the media jumped on the story. A native American claimed that he had tried to provide a peace barrier between the Catholic Highschool boys and a group of black Israelite protestors in front of the Lincoln Memorial. The video shows Nathan Phillips walk up face to face with a 16 year old boy, later identified as Nick Sandmann. Nick did not move or say anything just smiled. He was white and wearing a Red hat that said MAGA. He and fellow students had come from Kentucky annual march for pro-life. The story given by Phillips was that the boys were aggressive and they blocked his path and he felt afraid of the boys.

Nick and the other boys were immediately condemned based on Phillips account and the short video. Even their school criticized them as did several Catholic Bishops from Kentucky. The media and Democrats and left liberal entertainers piled on. Phillips portrayed himself as a tribal elder, a Vietnam Veteran, and a former Marine recon ranger. The criticism of the boys especially Nick escalated to doxing, threats of violence against Nick and other students.

Internet warriors came to the rescue. Within two days many considerate internet people found other videos that showed the boys did nothing wrong and Nick was simply trying to smile and stay cool and not let Phillips who had come with an entourage to provoke him. The story collapsed and the final outcome was Nick and his family hired attorneys who are now suing everyone including Nathan Phillips for defamation. This is a prime example of what internet warriors can do to set the record straight, help punish the "bad guys" and finally put the Democrats, and their left lib media in its place.

We need internet warriors to join with the Task Force to make the 2020 campaign the fairest election in modern times. If the Democrats and the media step over the line, they will find a tsunami come down on them. Nothing should go unresearched and unchallenged. If this is what you are already doing, keep at it. If you want to, jump in. All of you should know there is power in numbers so forming groups to work on specific topics or candidates is an advantage. Getting the word out, letting the public know what you know will be the challenge. Use networking. Join every social media you can and GET YOUR REPORT OUT. Join you tube and place your story online so it is not lost to the public.

### *Ad Hoc Committees for Research*
We would like to see some dedicated Patriots take up the task of in depth research of the "deep state" and the Democrat party. There are some groups doing a great job now but, we believe Red Wave Taskforce can provide a real impetus, as it is coupled with the excitement and energy of a presidential election. Also, the approach we propose is to include the "crowd funding" method to enhance data search. The more people hunting down information and studies, the quicker we will get all the information needed to make a report. With many people helping you will also have a ready base of people with an interest in getting the story out when the report is done.

Two places to start would be Judicial Watch and Openthebooks.com. We will have a longer list of resources in our appendix to this book. We will feature these projects on our website and ask that all who join the grassroots movement for a Red Wave victory to assist these ad hoc committees.

### Choose Your Own Mission

The above missions are suggestions and recommendations. As in any free grassroots movement the decision of what role to play or mission to take is not dictated to you but rather FREELY CHOSEN BY YOU. It should be an exciting time for all who love their country to know that there are roles they can take that will help ensure a victory on November 3, 2020.

# CHAPTER 2
# STRATEGY

The Strategy is basically a five-part approach to the entire campaign. They include the following:

1. Continuing Operation One: Keeping Elections Fair and Honest;
2. Continuing Operation Two: Register and Recruit
3. Continuing Operation Three: Winning the Hearts and Minds.
4. The Primary Elections;
5. The General Elections.

The first three operations continue from beginning until the general election is completed. We will deal with these three continuing operations in this chapter. Separate subsequent chapters will cover the Primary Election and the General election.

## CONTINUING OPERATION ONE:

### *Keeping the Elections Fair and Honest*

There is a reason almost half of the voter age population do not vote: many of them do not believe the elections are fairly run and free from fraud and cheating. One of the biggest fraud areas in the voting is by non-citizens. The Washington Times ran an article quoting from a study by a Political Scientist Jesse Richman of Old Dominion University, which estimated 800,000 non-citizen voters may have voted for Hilary Clinton in the 2016 presidential election. It is a criminal offense for non- citizens to vote in America (18USC Sec. 611). The penalty can be up to one year in prison and a fine. With the estimated number, you would expect to see more news articles about illegal voting by non-citizens. Keep watching news sources but also check out watch dog groups to learn the full extent of the voter fraud in America.

There is a lot the Taskforce can do to change that perception and encourage more voter participation. We should start with some very simple actions we need now. The author lives in South Carolina where there are certain voting laws in effect. First and most important is voter ID. You need picture ID to vote. There are also restrictions on mail in ballots and early balloting. Let's start here.

Everyone reading this book is guaranteed certain civil rights by the Constitution and its Amendments. Three very important ones will be discussed throughout the book. First, the right of free speech. Second, the right to petition the the government. Third, freedom of assembly and association.

Each Taskforce volunteer should make it his or her mission to write, email, telephone their congressperson and state legislators and DEMAND that voter ID be passed into law and that it be prominent in the issues in party platforms. Some of you can take this up as your mission during the campaign of 2020 and organize ongoing letter and email messages keeping this issue in the forefront of the elected officials, the electorate and the candidates. You may well find that a calling to stamp out voter fraud and fraud in elections is a Patriot mission you wish to take up. The following are some groups already at work in seeking elections free of fraud:

Judicial Watch
see www. Judicialwatch.org
Openthebooks.com


## CONTINUING OPERATIONN TWO:

## REGISTER AND RECRUIT

### *Have Faith in Our Youth*
We know many people are afraid that young people have a rebellious streak. They would almost automatically be drawn into the left lib side with its almost taboo adherence to anything counterculture. However, this

election provides us with a golden opportunity. Our obligations to educate the young also means to provide them with the knowledge of our political system and our American history. This election and their participation is just that opportunity.

The author of this book is a Vietnam Veteran. Last summer he accepted chairmanship of the scholarship committee of his local VFW unit. In the past there was little participation. The author contacted schools and teachers. He spoke directly to students in their classroom. The number of applicants in 2018 was huge. There was an essay contest called Patriots Pen and a recorded speech contest for high school students entitled Voice of Democracy.

The subject for Voice of Democracy throughout America in 2018 was "Why My Vote Matters." It was emotionally gratifying to hear the recordings of so many teenagers seriously spelling out why their vote counts in America. It immediately restored faith. The judging was done on November 11, 2018, and the author was one of the judges.

Before judging the essays and recordings, the author with a few veterans marched in the local Veteran's Day Parade. The two local high schools had sent Junior ROTC units in uniform to march as well. Over 80 young men and women had showed up to march and pay respect to the deceased Veterans. It was amazing and heartening. Not the picture we so often see about young people today. These young people should be encouraged to register and participate in upcoming elections. They are knowledgeable, dedicated and obviously have affection for their country.

Invite them to join in the campaign and ask them if they are of age to register and vote. Assist them and they will do just fine.


### *The Elderly*

You should see if all members of your family of voting age are registered to vote. One group often overlooked is the elderly. Many have transportation issues and some are in senior facilities. They still function very well and are some of the most motivated voters in America. Make sure that their registration is current and that they have a way to vote. Some states allow mailing ballots and others allow early balloting. A call to local registrar of voters will assist in finding the best way to help your elderly relatives and friends so they can also take part in the vote.

Be also on alert for the numerous efforts to exploit the elderly. There have been groups that go to senior retirement and care facilities offering to help seniors fill out ballots and deliver ballots for them. This is "Ballot harvesting." Warn your loved ones against this and make sure they vote without interference and their ballot is delivered properly.


### The Independents

"See how they love one another." (Tertullian of Carthage) The early Christian Church was in danger of being stamped out. Most religions at the time of the Roman Empire became popular at the point of a sword or spear. The Christians were speaking the gospel, but often ended up being burned or fed to the lions in the colosseum in Rome. Yet, after years of spreading the gospel and suffering persecution, the Roman Empire became converted to Christianity. The first Emperor to convert was Constantine. In 380 Christianity was made the official religion of the Roman Empire. A religion based on charity won over the violent and almighty Roman Empire. Winning the hearts and minds of voters does not take negative attacks. It is not "gotcha" and ambush politics. Its letting people know the good news of your platform and quality of your candidates.

The "independents" have answered surveys complaining that that the parties are too negative and interested in attacking each other. Well, give them the good news of your platform. Do not just spend time telling them how bad or evil the Democrats are. Let them know they should vote with you and the candidates who have solutions. Do not waste your time trying to convert a relative or friend who is a die-hard Democrat to vote for your candidates. Address the Independents and ask them to dialogue with you on the issues and candidates. You will win the heart and minds for November 2020.

### *Recruit the 44.3%*

VEP stands for Voter Eligible Population. CBS News did research that showed only 49 % of VEP voted in the midterm 2018 election. Presidential year elections are usually better attended. Even so research by Pew Research Center found that only 55.7% of VEP voted in 2016. Herein lies the greatest opportunity and prize of this election. If an all-out effort is made to bring these people back to the ballot box, there will not be a Red Wave victory, there will be a Red Tsunami.

Question is how to win the hearts and minds of the 44.3%? There is two parts to the answer. First you must find and identify the non-voters. Second you must convince them that their vote counts and is needed. We will address each issue.

1. Most people do not wear a sign saying they did not vote. They can be found very easily. When you work neighborhoods asking people to register and vote, you will know. When you go door to door with voter lists given you by your local Party or precinct captain, make note of the neighborhood with those not listed and see them anyway. Pass out literature. They may be a Democrat. But they may also be unregistered voters. Write the address and name if they give it to you down in your notebook for further contacting.

2, Many voters including those who voted in the past, feel the elections are either rigged or fraudulent, and many do not see how their one vote counts anyway. Be ready to show them. Research close elections. Show them the percentage of voters at elections. Let them know that one half of the voting population is voting to decide what the other half must do or not do. This is the greatest time for you to pitch why you love this country.

The most progress in winning the election is to recruit the people who have not voted. If you take up this mission, you will not only be assisting a Red Wave victory in November 2020, but you will be helping the political health of America.

## CONTINUING OPERATION THREE:

## WINNING THE HEARTS AND MINDS

### *Setting the Record Straight/ Getting the Message Out*

Ignorance and misunderstanding stands in the way of "winning hearts and minds." Often the way to a political victory is not in each candidate or each issue being won; but rather, it comes with winning the hearts and minds" of the electorate. They want to be a Republican. They want to be part of a "grassroots movement", that makes America Great Again. They have to accept it in their minds and in their hearts. They have to be shown facts that convinces their mind this is the Party and these are the candidates I should vote for and support. They must also feel in their hearts that it is the morally right thing to do as well.

The current method of the Democrats seems to be to attack the Republicans as voters and demean them and shame them and to attack the Party in general. We spoke of this when we discussed the Radical political philosopher Saul Alinsky. We make it clear that many of the Democrats are devotees of Alinsky, this includes Hilary Clinton. What you must understand that they, the Alinsky type Democrats already see us the mortal enemy. When someone says he is your enemy, TRUST HIS STATEMENT AND TAKE ACTION.

Start by showing the prospective voters why the Republican Party and its candidates should be supported and win the election. Do not start out negative, especially with independent and non-aligned voters. Tell them what is good about us, not what is bad about the Democrats. Stress the fact that the Republican Party was founded to end slavery in 1860. The Party has always been right on moral issues. The way to turn the tables on the Democrats is to do a comparison of the two parties' history. Several people on social media have provided charts showing a comparison of the history of both parties. A final chart should show the positions now taken by the Democrats as compared with the Republicans. It would be devastating. Every Taskforce Member should have these two charts and we would challenge some of you proactive voters to start working on the charts as part of your mission. Let us share with others including the Red Wave Taskforce website.

The Democrat Party and its candidates are the primary enemies for the November 3, 2020 election. You need to know everything about them you can. We suggest you might start by watching the documentary or reading the book written by conservative writer Dinesh D'Souza. The Title of the book and movie is "Death of a Nation: Plantation Politics and the Making of the Democratic Party." D'Souza gives us a factual history of the Democratic Party with contrast to the Republican party which won its first presidential election in 1860. To be an effective proactive voter, do educate yourself on the parties' history. It will assist when you are countering the attacks by the Democrats and left liberals. Each Taskforce person should have a chart made up that shows the historical events of the Republican Party and compared with Democrats history. People will be amazed how the Republican Party is the Party championing civil rights, and the Democrats have been the party that supported slavery, "Jim Crow" laws, opposition to the Civil Rights Act of 1964. This chart should be in your file whenever you go anywhere especially on "door knocking."

There are charts available on the internet similar to what we have proposed. You can use those but remember to verify the data. Use your own networking to get this information out and keep the record straight.

### Tell the Good News

Go to the official website of the Trump for 2020 campaign or go directly to the gop.com website, and look for the list of accomplishments by the Trump administration. It is impressive. President Trump accomplished more in his first two years than any other president in modern times.

People usually vote their pocketbooks, and when you can show voter the data on low unemployment, new job creation, salary gains and the economy continuing to boom, you will meet the first litmus test to getting someone to vote the Red Wave in 2020. Stay updated on the good news so you can honestly engage with the Voters with the good news.

Always look for some success that you can share with others. Be positive and people will want to join you. If the President concluded a trade agreement, let people know. If we have anything breaking that is good news spread the word by your own network system as you can believe the main media will not cover the event or story.

## Who We Are

Do not let the Democrats take the initiative at any time. Do not let them set the narrative on any subject or issue. All of us need to follow this one simple rule "Action not Reaction." Lead do not follow and be forced to counter the Democrats Do not always be on the defensive. The Democrats want to vilify and demonize not only Republican leaders but also Republican voters. They mock and they use Alinsky's favorite weapon: "ridicule."

A project some of you might take up is to form a group and do a website devoted to knowing WHO WE ARE. Feature the current office holders and tell their background. Feature stories about the rank and file Republicans. Show their diversity and that they all have in common is their love of country.

It's called "PR" and "branding" in the advertisement industry. If done factually correct and with an affirmative and positive attitude it will indeed make the Republican party and its candidates more appealing to all voters.

When independents and those who have not voted know the history of the Republican Party, our success in office, know the issues of the Party, and know who we are as Republicans, we will win the battle for their "hearts and minds."

# CHAPTER 3

# PRIMARY ELECTIONS

Most of us have heard people say after an election that they "…voted for the lesser of two evils." Many publicly decry their choices by saying "…why don't they get us better candidates to choose from." The rule generally is that the political parties before the primary refrain from sponsoring or endorsing primary election candidates. It is up to the electorate to take charge and bring forward the candidates.

It may well be that the primary elections are the most critical part of the campaign, not the general election. Many would argue, we are just not going to win general elections, if we do not obtain the very best candidates at the primaries. The "second string" just will not do.

Most of the work in primary elections is free lance unless you have decided to run as a candidate or you have volunteered someone else to do so. The following is something we would like all of you who are in on the Red Wave Taskforce to do.

1.  Sit down a make a list of people you believe should run for office and match it up with the list you have of offices up for election on Appendix A.
2.  Contact others like yourself and compare notes and see if you can come up with a short list of potential candidates.
3.  If you have a list, do not be afraid to approach the potential candidate and see if he or she is interested.
4.  Don't waste time with those who are not sure.
5.  Go as an ad hoc committee. There is an energy when the request comes from a group.

Have backup in mind in case the person backs out or vetting shows something that would preclude the person from office or make his election almost impossible (a criminal record etc.)

Do not just ask the person to run for office, offer that person your support and a Set a time and place for a first organizational meeting. Organizing a campaign for a candidate without interference from the government or anyone else is the most precious freedom we have. Use it.

Someone has to be in charge of the early process of getting on the ballot. At least one of the early steering committee must read the election rules. Read further in Chapter 6 we discuss further in depth. Just remember, your candidate cannot get elected if he or she does not make it onto the ballot.

The primary election is sometimes a "cake walk" especially when one party dominates a district or office. If there is an incumbent Republican who has announced he will again run for office, support him or her. The election of 2020 is NOT THE TIME TO TEST TERM LIMITS ISSUE by trying to oust a popular Republican office holder. You will most likely hand the election to a Democrat if it is a competitive race in the general election.

Sometimes it is better for a candidate to seek a different office. Some races in the primaries get overloaded with candidates and they beat each other up so bad that they have nothing left for the general election. For 2020, our goal is to take control of the United States Senate and the House of Representatives as well as the Presidency. If we put too many of our best candidates vying for one office and have few or none for others, we will defeat our purpose. Visit with the potential candidates and suggest they might pick another office where they may be needed. Sometimes first-time candidates "shoot for the moon." Often elected offices go empty or an incumbent has no opponent. If you are new at this, try for County Supervisor before you have visions of going to Washington D.C. as a congressman/woman or a senator. WE NEED TO FILL ALL OUR OFFICES WITH GOOD RESPONSIBLE CITIZENS.

Remember, we have three continuing operations and we should work diligently at those. They are part of "branding" the Republican party and the Red Wave Taskforce 2020 grass roots movement. You should contact people about the three continuing operations and add those people you meet to your notebook. When you see them again during the general election campaign, they will remember you and will probably assess you as a serious civic minded citizen. That is exactly what we want.

Lastly, do not let ANY PARTISAN position go without a Republican candidate in the primary. We are in all-out war mode and we cannot give up one elected position without a fight. If you try hard enough you could win the primary and with some momentum go on to be one of those newcomers who upset the favored rival.

We call upon you who have chosen to be the lone wolf garrison Taskforce member in your county, to step up and seek candidates. Then call for help. That is what the grassroots movement is for. No election without a Republican on the ballot.

# CHAPTER 4
# TACTICS AND PLANS

By now, many of you have probably underlined and written notes in this handbook. We want you to do just that, and it would help if you also took your notebook and started writing in it as you read. Tactics and plans chapter will be filled with so many ideas and suggestions that you should take notes.

## *Caveat*

There is no question that after the last presidential election, the political and campaign environment has become confrontational and toxic. The vitriol and often assaults on people who are just wearing a MAGA hat are now legion. The protests in the streets by ANTIFA are legion. The harassment on college campuses of Republicans and conservatives is heartbreaking but an epidemic. Watching elected officials harassed and bullied out of restaurants and other public places is scandalous and upsetting.

If you fear the confrontation aspects of door to door campaigning or being bullied in public places and tense public activities, you can still join the Movement and adapt to the suggestions we made for the more housebound persons. You can still make telephone calls, email, social media blogging, stuffing envelopes and other necessary work can be done from the office or your home. Do try however some of the less stressful events such as meet the candidate at a home party.

A number of us are war veterans. We really believe that it was worth it to risk life and limb for all Americans right to free speech and to vote. We are sure most of you feel a little uncomfortable but that is not too high a price in comparison to pay for being a member of the Red Wave Taskforce 2020

We do want you to be safe and free from as much stress as possible. We have provided these guidelines to assist you.

1. Try to go to events with a partner and in fact three is not a crowd but safety;
2. Always bring at least two smart phones with you to record audio and video in conflict situations and also to document anything of importance;
3. Smart phone should be set for 911 speed dial;
4. Use all other safety precautions and report incidents and things that appear Unlawful or disturbing.
5. Let someone know where you are going and when you plan to return.
6. Stay safe but stay resolved to do your part as well.

### *Home Based Warriors*

While living in Colorado, the author of this book received a telephone call from a senior citizen lady living in Michigan. She was calling to find people who would make calls on behalf of Scott Brown as the Republican candidate for Senator in a special election in Massachusetts. She was a homebased warrior to be sure. The election on January 19, 2010 made Scott Brown senator in an upset victory. Brown was aided immensely by Tea Party Groups and many grass roots people anxious to help elect more Republicans and fiscal conservatives to office. The lady from Michigan shows what a person who seems more confined to home can do and still make a difference.

### *Boycotts and other Pressure Tactics*

Remember to keep our eyes on the prize: winning the elections in November 2020. We have learned that the independent voters and the 43% unregistered voters are turned off on negative campaigning. So, we have a balancing that must be done. We have seen the Democrats and the left liberals engage in "gotcha" politics. Then they start a stampede to make people resign from office or resign from their jobs, especially as talk show celebrities and newscasters.

We should not shy away from such tactics but use only in extreme situations. The best move is to use a counter-tactic when the Democrats and other avowed libs try to steamroll a boycott or pressure a resignation. A few years back LBGT groups and many lib Democrats as well as the news media, were expressing support for the boycott called against the Chick-fil-A restaurants. The public came in mass support of the restaurant and the boycott only accomplished raising the restaurant's revenue. The bully groups have a free speech right to call for a boycott but we also have a right to call for a counter move to blunt the boycott.

Pressure tactics and boycotts are often counterproductive. They can be used and should be in the most pressing situations where the opponents have overreached or are trying to "spin" a false or exaggerated story. Seek a lot of council before calling for pressure tactics such as boycotts or demands for resignation.

### *What is Moral? / Setting the Narrative*

Nancy Pelosi calls President Trump's wall immoral. She does not call the abortion at birth (actually infanticide) immoral. She is following the protocols set out in futuristic books like *Brave New World* and "1984." They let us know that you can flip old morality as the immorality. Hypnopaedia, political correctness, school children indoctrination and soon we believe up is down and down is up. Finally, moral is whatever I say it is and can scream the loudest.

She, like so many Democrats, have been schooled in the political philosophy of Saul Alinsky and his primer for radicals. Tell a major lie long enough and people will ultimately come to believe it. That is one of the tactics from all radicals who cannot legitimately win your heart and mind with logic and facts. Turn the light of truth on them when they try to engage in this "dirty trick." AND DON'T ANY OF YOU TRY THIS. BELIEVE WHAT YOU SAY AND SAY WHAT YOU REALLY BELIEVE

### *Face Time Better Than Facebook Time*

Up close and personal is the best way to win a potential voter. Internet communications can be very impersonal and at time deceiving. We are human beings and we are equipped to meet people face to face, shake hands and enjoy each others company. This goes too for political campaigns. The people want to see and hear the candidate, not just watch the candidate on a screen. Check out the massive rallies for Donald Trump. He is the master at the extended face time rally. He knows this is how you win people over. Copy this for yourself and get candidates you work with to hold rallies, coffees, and simple door to door events.

Consider bringing your children with you. Make it a learning experience and show how important you feel the campaign is to you by bringing your family to meet the citizens at their homes. We know that not everyone is outgoing, many find it hard to meet people. Maybe we should hold some workshops on this activity. Just let us know.

### *Who Is Saul Alinsky and Why Do We Care?*

In her senior year of college Hillary Clinton wrote a thesis on political philosopher Saul Alinsky. Alinsky had corresponded with Hillary Rodham (Clinton) offering her a job. She did not take the job, but went onto law school. Its been obvious over the years that many prominent Democrats and many of the Democrat base have taken up and followed Alinsky's philosophy for action. He coined the concept of the community organizer as the ultimate political activist. But it is his rules for radicals that set out the blueprint for the success of smaller groups of left liberal activists to gain political power through their adherence to Alinsky's tactics.

We have set out the Saul Alinsky's 13 Rules for Radicals and 11 Rules of Ethics and Means , which are excerpted from Saul Alinsky's book: *Rules for Radicals,* published in 1971, in Appendix D in this book. It is important to know the enemy's playbook if you want to defeat him. Reading these rules and seeing how the Democrats think and operate goes a long way to do just that.

One rule that Democrats seem to forget and therefore can be exploited is: "people who live in glass houses should not throw rocks at others." Whenever, Democrats go on a personal attack frenzy, know that they also have a closet and skeleton there. Go after them without fear. DO HOWEVER MAKE SURE YOU ARE NOT SLIPPING INTO THE FAKE SCANDAL SYNDROME. Sometimes people in a frenzy will start manufacturing scandals or exaggerating a circumstance to seem like a scandal. We do not do that or condone it. We do however, support calling out and going after candidates with scandals as it goes to their ability to serve.

Rule 5 of Rules for Radicals is as follows: "Ridicule is man's most potent weapon." Anyone who watched the Brett Kavanaugh senate committee hearings, knows this rule was in play by all the Democrats at the hearing. No attempt to be gracious or polite, the Democrats dripped with sarcasm and obvious disdain for Judge Kavanaugh. They engaged in questioning and techniques no judge would allow in a courtroom for any witness. The Democrats are merciless and many of the witnesses they used at the hearing turned out to be false and phony. We can use a similar tactic but with more responsibility and in keeping with our desire to be fair and honest in our campaign. If someone deserves calling out for scandal, an issue problem, or a character failure, then by all means make the message clear and broadcast to as many people as possible. Do not let up especially if it is a serious matter such as Hilary's lost emails. Return to the subject often. You take your lead from someone like President Trump. He is relentless.

During the 2016 campaign primary, Trump found himself constantly being attacked and ridiculed by the press and by other candidates. If you noticed he did not start off attacking them but they made the fatal mistake of trying to ridicule and shame Trump out of the race. No one has ever shown himself a master of the political counterattack as Donald J. Trump. He would look at his adversary and determine what their weakness was and then he would label that person. He would repeat that label over and over again until almost everyone in America knew who "little Marco" was or "Crooked Hilary" and "Crazy Bernie."

### *The Largest Medium for the Message*

According to Nielsen ratings and other survey companies, 93% of adults listen to radio every week but watch television 87%. Campaigns mean nothing if you do not get your message out to the public. Advertisement costs during elections can be enormous. We are trying to bootstrap a grassroots movement and want to make what money we spend count. Compare all advertisement mediums but do not pass up the obvious. People listen to radio.

The other advantage is that the stations running your ad is directing right at your market. You want to reach your voters in your district not waste a local election ad on people many miles away who will not be voting in your local election. Except for statewide races or the Presidential race all other elections are basically local.

Local radio will assist you in doing the ads. Also, there are small ad firms that can give you a high-quality audio ads, at reasonable cost. You might approach a few other Task Force patriots and talk about setting up a small funding program where you pay for the cost of the radio time as a way to encourage use of the radio for more candidates. Let the candidate and his group determine the content of the message. You are just facilitating so the ad gets to the public. That is not to say, you may have special skills in advertisement and may want to donate some work for small campaigns as well.

### *Dirty Tricks are Counterproductive and often Illegal*

Trick, lie, corruption is not what a democracy or any form of people empowered political system should ever be. We can win with the truth and with perseverance. When you sully the process with cheating " you sully the process." Win at all costs may be okay for some on the left liberal side, but it should never be with us. We want to claim the moral high ground. Here is our chance. Stay clean and call out the Democrats when they do not.

Also, there has been a push lately by watchdog groups for law enforcement to get more involved in policing fraud and corruption in the voting and campaign process. Better to always stay on the right side of the law.

### *It Should be in the Plans*

Every campaign should have plans to reach the goal of the campaigns. The goal for candidates is first to win the primary election. If they win the primary election, then their goal is to win the election on November 3, 2019. The plan includes the overall strategy but also the specifics such as tactics. Most of you will not be involved in specific campaigns and will not need the detailed planning they must do.

One thing to remember, as important as plans are, there are times when you must react because of some unforeseen event. You must be able to meet an immediate challenge. If you have chosen a mission or a project, you are in the best position to pivot and address a new and bigger challenge. This is true because we hope that you have constantly been kept up to date on anything that pertains to your project or mission. We also know that you can only respond quickly, if you continue to educate yourself on the subject matter.

Plans should be referenced to a currently updated calendar. Everything is time sensitive, most of all the election dates. Work your plan back from the important dates. This will also allow you a chance to always be in "action not reaction." Our opponents will then always be reacting to us. Always take the initiative and keep momentum on your side.

We are considering a workshop on tactics and planning and would appreciate your feedback.

# CHAPTER 5

# TOTAL WAR AND NO MANS LAND

In the elections of 2016 and 2018, we saw many party groups including the Republican National Committee make a decision that a certain candidate cannot win an election and withdrew any further funding. They sent those withheld funds to a contested race elsewhere. The abandoned candidate is now for all intents a dead candidate. His party has abandoned him. This is a huge mistake. Measured response tactics never work. By signaling you are admitting defeat in one race, your opponent now feels free to also take funds from the admitted race and use those funds for the more contested race. You have really gained nothing by the tactic of abandonment and marshalling of forces.

2020 is not just a skirmish or battle, it will be an all-out war. We need to campaign it as such. When you are outnumbered, lost your support, and you are surrounded….:" there is only one thing you can do -ATTACK" (Thomas Stonewall Jackson). If you learn a Republican candidate for the general election is being abandoned, sound the alarm. The Red Wave Taskforce never abandons a a fellow patriot. Contact the candidate's campaign and offer to help. Then contact and bulletin every Taskforce person you can find to engage in a "surge." Flood the candidate's area with phone calls, neighborhood door to door campaigning, meet the candidate parties, public rallies, and increased mailer activity.

Two things positive will come from this approach. One, you may just cause an upset election. Two, at least you will hold the Democrats to the battleground with a fear of moving money and resources to another contested area. In political campaigns as in real war, momentum can be everything. Never let the momentum move to the opponents. Always seize the initiative.

### Mass and Momentum (Cloudcrowd)

Most of us know what the term "flash mob" means. This simple but effective social experience has given rise to some new uses of the internet and other tech services. One example would be "crowdfunding." The internet has made it possible to unite thousands and at times hundreds of thousands of people to accomplish a single simple goal. It could be to meet at one place for a social event, or it might be to send money to fund some project.

We intend to have "cloudcrowds" to support campaigns. We will do our part to facilitate calls for "cloudcrowds" but would ask that all involved be of good will and not abuse the system. We are looking for feedback on this concept and practical solutions to facilitate a well-organized protocol. A massing of people and effort in a campaign can change morale and momentum immediately.

### Hit them again, hit them again, harder

Compare the Hilary email scandal with what was done and what should have been done for an example. The media was reluctant to do heavy reporting on the unfolding story of one of the worst scandals in modern American history. What should have been done is a constant reporting on every aspect of the issue. Most of us just sat back and saw such an obvious violation of law by Hilary and her aides that we expected the FBI, the DOJ and the media would get on top of this scandal. Remember, many said not "if" Hilary got indicted but rather "when" she would get indicted. The whole thing was sabotaged by Hillary supporters inside the FBI and DOJ and the media tried to spin the scandal the whole time. Here is what would happen if there was a Red Wave Taskforce:

1. All Taskforce would be contacted to partake in a total campaign to get rid of Hillary as a candidate and be the subject of a criminal investigation;
2. Every member would be asked to send emails, telegrams, telephone calls to Congress, the news media, the Department of Justice, the Democrat Party to remove Hilary from the ballot and open a

criminal investigation;

3. Members would be asked to form ad hoc committees to prepare and conduct investigations and research into the email and other Hilary scandals and make their research known on social media and through networking ;

4. All members would file FOIA (Freedom of Information Act) requests with FBI and the DOJ regarding the emails, and other scandals.

5. If the pressure does not bring results, there would be a night rally scheduled across America so the public could announce their wishes and speak with one voice.

That was then and conjecture. This is now. Hopefully, the work of watch dog groups and action groups such as ours will not throw another major scandal in this election cycle. If it does, we need a "blanket " approach. As many persons as we can should be working on the scandal and everyone will engage in "cloudcrowd" efforts. No way will a TRUE and SERIOUS scandal be left to others and squandered.

## Garrisons and Outposts

The Patriots of the Revolutionary War did not abandon any area of the colonies to the British Forces. Even those areas considered more loyal to the crown, such as Charles Town, South Carolina were not abandoned. A Patriot came forward, Francis Marion who became known as the "swamp fox." He made the life of General Cornwallis miserable. He would attack wagon trains, small outpost using raiding tactics. He is an example of the effort of one Patriot can have in a larger war.

If you live in a county that is overwhelmingly Democrat and you have the strength and character to establish a Republican garrison outpost there, then our hats are off to you. Just remember that you are not alone. Call for help and others will come. Let us know who you are and what you need. Keep everyone posted.

Your first effort should be to determine all positions that are up for election in the county you are the outpost. Make contact with each campaign and let them know you want to help and how you can contact others like yourself to give a hand in campaigning as well. Let us know who you are so we can let others know when you call for help.

Recruit a fellow Patriot and start walking the neighborhoods. This is the best way to show our presence and participation in the coming elections. This kind of campaigning is the hardest but most rewarding. We have seen districts turn around in campaigns when just one candidate walked his district over and over.

### *Example Script for "Door to Door"*

The most effective campaigns include the much heralded "door to door", "boots on the ground" face to face old fashion campaigning. This is especially true if you have elected to be one of the over 3000 county garrisoned leaders for the Red Wave Taskforce. Many people are skilled at personal meetings and many are a bit shy knocking on doors. Here is some help.

Try to go in pairs. It helps with those who are a little shy and it is more impressive when meeting the resident at his door. what you want to do is script the meetings with residents. The following is a model script, but we recommend that in time and with experience you should write your own script. These scripts should be practiced and should become your routine. Having a protocol takes away the shyness and provides confidence when doing your presentation.

### MODEL SCRIPT

"Hello, my name is Bob Smith. I am a volunteer with Red Wave Taskforce 2020. Here today to get some information to you about the election coming up on November 3, 2020. We are also asking residents to give their input on the Candidates issues and the campaigns." [ let the resident respond here.] If the resident is aggressive or even combative make the following statement: "I can see you are very committed to your candidates and party and that should help make this election campaign a spirited one. Thank you for your time" [ then leave] If the resident is friendly and willing to listen continue and hand the resident a list of candidates on their coming ballot.

"Here is a list of all the Republican candidates you will see on your ballot. We are also asking voters what issues are most important to them." [ hand the resident a list of the major issues of the campaign] "I can respond to some of your concerns including where to register to vote." [Take time to talk with the resident. Ask him if he would like to meet any of the candidates and if it would help to have the candidates come door to door to meet him and his neighbors. When you leave write down the address and name. This person is now your contact, and he can be sent a mailer or you can provide a candidate with his name and address for a future meeting.]

### It's Not Just About the Money

The midterm election in 2018 for the senatorial seat held by incumbent Ted Cruz went down as one off the most expensive senate campaigns in American History. Although Beto O'Rourke received $80,000,000.00 in donations to Ted Cruz receiving about $38,000,000.00, Cruz still won the election. This is contra to the more recent beliefs that he or she who has the largest cash war chest will win the election. Having a good candidate with a good platform on the issues, can win the election, especially if the money is replaced with hard work by volunteers.

Let's be clear. There is an amount of money, absolutely necessary to stay in the campaign starting with filing fees. With regulations now imposed on reporting and record keeping there is a need to hire experts.

# CHAPTER 6
# MODEL CAMPAIGN ORGANIZATION

All over America, thousands of people will soon "toss their hats in the ruing" and file to run for political office. From local councils and administrative positions, to state and federal higher offices, 2020 will be one of the largest protracted election events in the history of the world. However, it is not the "world cup", not the "world series", and not the "super bowl." No, it will be one of the most important events in world history. It will be free people from the most common man and woman making decisions about power, leadership and the direction of this country. It will be the largest mass power shift ever, without war or violence.

What will be the challenge is whether a mass of people can rule themselves. It should be noted that most of the candidates have little or no experience in politics, campaigns or holding office. Some of these candidates will be convinced that if they get some big donors they can literally purchase the election. Others believe that if they hire the right "professionals" they can easily win over the grassroots. Recent events in 2016 and 2018 have seemed to contradict this thinking. The public is tired of the "professionals"; slick "gotcha" negative campaigns and heavy cash infused war chests. Many surveys have found lower voter turnout has been caused in part by the perception that the elections are for sale. This book is about empowering you the grassroots, to take back the election process and have it function as it was meant to be-to express the real will of the people. Let's do that in 2020.

We covered earlier the need for good candidates and we now focus on that whole process from selection to model campaign organization. The person who decides who runs IS YOU. If you have serious intent to seek office, we provide a step by step process to help you decide.

1. Spend some time reflecting and researching the position you seek. Inner soul searching about your strengths and weaknesses as a leader and as communicator. Be brutally honest with yourself. Review any misdeed in your life that could come back to embarrass you or your family. Review your finances and make sure you can sustain a campaign and a time in office. Even when you feel you are okay to go ahead-stop and pray if you are religious or reflect again.

2. Next have an open discussion with your spouse or partner if you have one. A campaign and office is a big disruptor in children's lives and they also may not like the spotlight on a parent running for office which also reflects on them.

3. Next contact three people whose opinions and character you feel are above reproach. Ask each individually for their honest opinion on you seeking political office.

4. Then spend some time alone, reflecting and praying if you are a religious person. Once you have decided, let everyone know your decision and give it your all. Then decide and follow through with confidence and energy and a sense of purpose.

Immediately let everyone know you are deciding to run for office. Ask the three advisors to stay as advisors but also if any of them wish to be part of campaign staff. Have a list of positions to fill for your campaign staff and start writing names and phone numbers.

## Basic Staff

We have used a comparison to military staffing and will continue here:

1. Candidate;
2. Campaign manager;
3. S-1 Adjutant and Finance;
4. S-2 Intelligence and Counterintelligence;
5. S-3 Plans and Operations;
6. S-4 Material and Supplies

CAMPAIGN MANAGER: The most trusted person in your campaign. This person must be able to speak for you with the press or others when you are absent. The manager must be trusted with all confidential information. Pick wisely and do not be afraid to replace if you made a mistake in choosing your first manager.

S-1. ADJUTANT AND FINANCE: It would be nice if an attorney or an accountant volunteered for this position. This staff person is responsible for filing all the official documents necessary for the campaign, S1 has to set up the Campaign checking account so as to provide a perfect paper trail for all finances and donations. S1 must keep all records and see that the accounting books and ledgers are kept. This is one time you might want to consider spending some of your donations hiring an attorney and an accountant for consultation and assistance. Do obtain the election laws for the state you are in and the national election laws regarding finance and donations.

In 1972 the Congress passed the Federal Election Campaign Act. (52 U.S.C. Section 30101) This was done to primarily regulate campaign spending and fund raising. In 1974 the Act was amended to institute a Federal Elections Commission. The commission pre-empt any local or state elections laws when the election is for a federal office. We have provided a resource and research list to assist you in Appendix E. We can consider a workshop on this, BUT YOU REALLY SHOULD NOT WAIT BUT RESEARCH AND GET PERSONAL HELP. There are fines for failing to report or report incorrectly. These various rules not only can hurt with fines, our opponents can and will use any notice of violation by the FEC as some kind of proof of wrongdoing.

Check the state election codes as they also, have laws and regulations regarding financing and donations as well as other rules regarding campaigns. Research them as well.

The S-1 should also be responsible for personnel. Unless engaged as private contractors, you should not hire anyone as an employee. The laws you must obey and the regulations you must adhere to, can be problematic. Most of your help are strictly volunteers. You should have a disclaimer sheet, for people who are working with you that they understand they are not employees and that despite that fact your campaign does not discriminate on the basis of "sex, age, gender, ethnicity, religion, marital status, or any other type discrimination that is considered legally taboo." Make sure they understand your campaign will not tolerate discrimination nor will you allow any sexual or other misconduct to occur at the headquarters or any event of the campaign. Place the disclaimer in your headquarters on a bulletin board. Better, get legal advice from a local attorney about this.

S-2 INTELIGENCE/COUNTERINTELLIGENCE: In this modern era of high tech and "gotcha politics," Intelligence work may make or break a campaign.

Intelligence is an effort to gather data about a person, an issue, or an institution and draw a conclusion from the analysis of the data. The first dossier the S-2 staff should assemble and report is on their own candidate. No surprises later as we have already discussed. The next dossier should be a research of the opponent candidates. These two dossiers should be updated and be shown only to the Candidate and the Campaign manager.

Good intelligence requires endless search and researching to keep current on the political situation. We have placed some liberal and conservative websites in Appendix F to assist you to stay informed. The key word is "all source" in intelligence. Check every information source possible to get the true picture. Any new event that could impact your candidate should be brought to his attention immediately.

The S-2 also provides counterintelligence and security for the candidate. Security can sometimes mean obtaining security guards. However, you most important responsibility is to protect the candidate. Deflect attacks by opponents, the press and others. AND ALWAYS counterattack/" pushback." No attack ever goes unanswered.

The opponents sometimes will send you volunteers who are spies. Be on the watch and do most of your discussions on serious matters with just a small trust group. Also, watch for "leakers." Some people cannot help but tell all. Leaks can derail a campaign.

S-3 PLANS AND OPERATIONS: These are the people who run the calendar and map out and plan the campaign. They are also persons who do up the official press releases and position statements. They assist in prepared speeches for the candidate. It would help if at least one Staff 3 member was a good speech writer.

It is very important that only the Candidate and the campaign manager EVER speak or release statements on behalf of the candidate. This should be made clear to the entire staff and all volunteers. If they want to talk about a released statement fine, but not just give a statement about what they believe the candidate would say. Many campaigns have had to "walk back" statements because too many diverse people were speaking on behalf of the candidate. Make sure the volunteers do not become self-appointed spokespeople for the campaign. S-4 MATERIAL AND SUPPLIES: The logistics staff is underrecognized but absolutely critical. This staff is in charge of supplies, the office, ordering signs banners, food, and more. They arrange meeting halls, transportation and put together work crews.

In all cases try to find at least two people for each staff position. Campaigns are voluntary and there often is a high turnover rate for campaign workers. If you need help send out a call to the Taskforce and ask for some help. We don't want to see any campaign suffer from lack of volunteers. This is a grassroots movement with a chance for many qualified people to have a good chance to win the elections.

# CHAPTER 7

# GENERAL ELECTION

The final battle of course is the General Election. It will be waged over every inch of American soil in 2020. When an area of operation is this large, many strategists will try and reduce their coverage and concentrate all their efforts where they believe they will have the most success. As we have stated, this is total war and conceding victories right from the start is never a winning strategy.

The United States is made up of 3142 counties (per worldatlas.com) including districts called parishes. The plan is to garrison a presence in each and every county. This is where the Red Wave Taskforce can be most effective. We call for Pick up the flag and plant it in your county. It will be more of an outpost if you happen to live in a total "blue" county. It just means you will have more impact and will take them on with the element of "surprise."

## D-DAY: Final Offensive

The Democrat party has traditionally used Labor Day as a time for picnics and rallies to support their candidates by also showing their support for labor in America. As of the 2016 election, it appears that labor now prefers Donald Trump, a Republican. It is for this reason, we selected September 7, 2020 as D-Day for the last surge and political offensive in the run up to the General Election on Tuesday November 3, 2020.

We will be publishing on our website notices about this last campaign offensive often as we get close to D-Day. What we are looking for is a grand full- scale effort by everyone who identifies with our grassroots movement. We would like you to share your ideas and recommendations as well. For now, our general is as follows:

1. Each Task Force person should have stored material for this last push to include campaign literature, poster, house signs, bumper stickers.
2. A copy of the list of candidates always with you and copies to pass out.
3. A list of the accomplishments of the current administration with copies to pass out.
4. A telephone number and a website address for people to check so they can find out if registered and how and where to vote
5. Each person should try and host a meet the candidate picnic or barbeque at home or a park and if not try and find one to attend. These are set for Labor Day. (our D-Day)
6. The day before Labor Day use your network "cloudcrowd" notifications about D-Day and where the persons are needed for a picnic, rally or the like.

Enjoy Labor Day as it will be fun and exciting. If you have children, bring them with you to the rally or picnic you plan to attend as well. Try to attend a rally where there will be candidates present. Make sure everyone knows you are excited about the homestretch.

Since you have planned for D-Day, you have hit the ground running and know what your next step will be. Our opponents may not have planned much beyond simply attending a Labor Day event. To us this is kick off time.

Remember, D-Day is Labor Day and that is September 7, 2020. This leaves very little campaign time, as the general election is November 3, 2020. With early voting allowed and mailed in ballots, we can only get maximum campaign exposure up to October 7, 2020. Our audience of potential voters get smaller each day after that, as early ballots and mail-in ballots start to be sent.

That is why the Taskforce should have prepared a number of envelopes with the campaign literature from every Republican candidate running in your county. You should have obtained mailing addresses from Central Committee or purchased them from address collecting companies. The envelopes would constitute a mailing for the general public. Then mail out as much as you can.

If you do not want to do your own mailer pack, contact the county Republican Central Committee and volunteer to stuff envelopes for a final mailer in your county. Even better, would be you take your packages and return to the neighborhoods and hang the packages on doors or deliver directly to residents. We want to achieve the wave affect of a last run of campaign material being handed out. It gives momentum to the Red Wave and a morale shock to our opponents.

This last segment of time should include replacing signs and finding places for new ones. Time to pass out more bumper stickers. Time to contact everyone in your phone and internet list concerning the election.

### *Red Hat Day*

October 19, 2020 is tentatively set for "red hat" day. The word will go out "cloudcrowd" type so that all Taskforce and all persons wanting a Red Wave victory on November 3, 2020 will participate. We would like to see everyone wear a red hat (better yet one that has MAGA written on it) on this day in support of the President and all Republican candidates. What Democrats and independents will see that day is a sea of Red Hats. In their hearts they will feel a Red Wave will follow.

We know that for some of you this is very daunting. Many have seen videos of people being harassed or even assaulted while wearing a Red MAGA hat. We do not want you to be harmed or even harassed simply to exercise your first amendment rights. It could be made easier if you bring your hat and put it on while at a set rally or even a "honk and wave" event. There is safety in numbers. We would ask everyone to assist setting up a spontaneous rally or preplanned on October 19 and then get the word out by social media, emails, telephone.

If there is huge success, we will call for another Red Hat day. It may be that most of you will not feel intimidated and opt to wear the hats more often without need of a special day. Feedback would help.

### *It's Not Over until the Votes are Counted*

The election is not over on November 3, 2020. There is a lot of work to be done and it is important. We hope that many of you volunteered to act as polling officials or participate in the vote count. This is by far the best way to watch for and insist the election process remains free of fraud or deceit. The Republican party is also entitled in most states to have official poll watchers. Volunteer for this position as it is the quickest way to challenge any impropriety or out and out cheating during the Election process.

For those of you who have finished on election day, go to one of the candidate or party headquarters to watch the returns. Take pride in yourself and what you did to make the election happen and get the results we all wanted.

# CHAPTER 8

# ISSUES, POLICIES AND PLATFORM

Two elements make up the decision of voters at elections: the candidate and the issues he espouses. At times, one element is more important than the other. With the grave importance of the 2020 election, we should strive for the very best candidates and the key issues of most concern to voters. We spoke at length about the importance of selecting the best candidates in the primary. Once the candidates are selected, we are stuck with them. We may have let the "second-string" carry the ball if, we did not heed the warning to concentrate on recruiting top candidates.

Here we reflect on issues and policies and how they can shape and many times make or break a campaign. Issues are the individual concerns of the electorate that candidates and parties address with a solution and method of dealing with that issue. The platform is the candidate's or the party's listing of issues and the standard response to those issues. We list the issues we believe will be the most important ones for 2020, if not in the mind of the candidates, we believe in the minds of the electorate.

We also encourage you alone or with some other proactive voters take on one or more of these issues to be the advocate for the issues based on the platforms of the party and our candidates. You will need to become expert in these issues but your most important function would be to get the message out so that the issue is part of the campaign process and the electorate knows what our position is. If we do this we will win. The method to get the message out we discussed in the chapter on tactics.

*1. The Economy.*

There is an old saying: "the voters always vote their pocketbooks." If this is the overriding issue, there will be a Red Wave landslide on November 3, 2020. Every member of the Taskforce should keep updated copies of the Trump administration successes. You will find data on the lowest unemployment rates ever in America with the highest employments of all times. Make sure to get the word out as the main media is anti-Trump and anti-Republican. A success on the economy is not a success if the word does not get out to the vast majority of the people. So, when you learn good news spread it.

## *2. Abortion.*

What may be the key issue in 2020 may well be the issue that has been around since the decision of *Roe v. Wade* by the Supreme Court. It seems the issue had been ended with the decision but then the question arose "at what time was the fetus viable and a person by legal definition." Two events have recently happened which has absolutely returned the issue to the forefront in America.

First, on May 13, 2013 Kermit Gosnell, M.D. was convicted of three counts of murder in Pennsylvania. He was convicted of delivering babies and completing abortions after delivery. The description of the killings were so horrific Dr. Gosnell was sentenced to life without parole. The jury had called the destruction of babies in this way as infanticide, baby murder.

On January 22, 2019, the Democrats in New York passed a "Reproductive Health Act, making abortions through the third trimester legal if it was determined in the best interests of mother to abort. No end limit was put on termination so it could take place up to the moment of delivery. Nothing was really determined if the abortion was actually started by delivery then destruction of the new born as sort of a "partial birth abortion." The legislation could allow for someone like Gosnell to engage in the acts he was doing for what a jury determined was murder. However you look at this, many people do consider this a law allowing infanticide.

Trump predicted September 26, 2016 that the laws for abortion would soon allow a baby to be ripped out of the womb at nine months. This effort to condone killing unwanted babies is with the Democrat party. They cheered for it; they have opposed laws that would require doctors to protect a baby born alive after a failed abortion; and have generally opposed every effort to protect innocent life.

We again need ad hoc committees to work up a complete study on this issue and then flood the populace with our findings. Then we need to call out the Democrats on this issue. Since the issue is 84% opposed to the third trimester abortions, the Democrats could see a sizable loss of voters in 2020 over this issue alone. Once the issue is publicized, we must not relent but continuously hammer the opposition with it.

### 3. Immigration.

The Democrats have in the last few years locked into this as probably their major issue. Their position is not strong even though they believe it is. For example, Senator Schumer and Congresswoman Pelosi just a few years back, were demanding that we build barriers and fences to keep out illegal immigrants. They insisted that more should be done to deport illegals who were draining our government funds for assistance and welfare. Now they have taken a 180 degree turn and are demanding just the opposite.

Today the Democrats appear to be for the following:

1.  Open borders;
2.  Relaxed criteria for refugee asylum;
3.  Extraordinary government benefits for illegals and their children such as Free college tuition, free medical care, attorney services by "sanctuary state California", and tax refunds for head of household even if illegal in the country and did not pay any taxes.

Most polls and surveys show the American public wants border security and are not happy with so much money given in preference to illegal immigrants and refugees.

The Democrats are trying to downplay the harm done to the country and make it a moral issue. Well, there is a moral issue and it is on the side of those who oppose illegal immigrants and the Democrats who exploit them politically.

We need Patriots from Taskforce to start ad hoc committees to research and collect absolute data on the harm of the illegal immigrants. We need to chart the percentage of prisoners in America who are illegal immigrants. We need to chart the total of violent crime and the attacks and murders of law enforcement. They need to verify the list of sanctuary cities and states. Document the services provided to illegals and the efforts of elected officials to thwart ICE and other Federal agencies.

A plan to make these immigration issues one major political issue is necessary. Besides making everyone aware, some pressure should be brought to the table. All Democrats should be called upon to declare if they support open borders and sanctuary cities.

Next, we should work with the Angel Moms who have gotten little publicity. These are the ones who have lost children and relatives to illegal immigrant violent crimes. Take their message to the Democrats who are trying to ignore it. Next petition the DOJ to bring criminal charges against the local officials who obstruct justice and lend aid and comfort to criminals to evade capture.

Lastly, most states have statutes that allow "taxpayer lawsuits." This is where the taxpayer brings an action against a government official or entity for misuse of public funds. Consult an attorney if you go this route. In most cases the misused funds are used to give free education to illegal immigrants, free attorney services in California, and other expenditures to aid and abet and obstruct Federal law.

The next step is to get the word out. A complete report should be sent everywhere including the main media as well as all elected officials. Then, make contact with the "Angel Moms" and support an ongoing series of rallies and protests to confront the Democrats over the harm done by sanctuary cities. Democrats have shown a brutal callousness of avoiding the Angel Moms. This can be an effective campaign tactic in 2020. ANGEL MOMS PROJECT call for ad hoc committees to draw up charts and a full data checked report so there is no question as to the basis of their complaint and the nations complaint of sanctuary cities. Then publish the report and hold rallies and protests until November 3, 2020.

### 4. National Security

We have seen the spectacle of leaders of the Federal Government national security agencies, law enforcement and intelligence communities openly criticize and condemn the national security policies of the President. The President, however, is the only elected official authorized by the constitution to set and administer national security. Our form of government empowers elected officials with the authority to set and administer this policy. The Senate does have some control as they must approve treaties. But the bureaucracy of even the highest administrators are NOT AUTHORIZED to set our policy and not authorized to discredit the president or try to set up a secret rebellion to disregard the President's directions. These bureaucrats do not like the policy they should run for office or resign your position and speak out publicly as is your right.

Again ad hoc committees are sought to do complete study on national security which should provide a history of President Trump's efforts and successes in handling national security. Example, there have been no missile testing by North Korea since President Trump was elected and ISIS is almost totally destroyed.

### 5. Taxes and Government Spending.

Taxpayer groups have been around for years sounding the alarm about taxes and the out of control spending. We have a few of these groups in our resource section in the Appendix F. You should contact these groups or at least see their websites so you can speak with some knowledge on the issue. Be sure to get a copy of the latest Tax law and/or a synopsis so you can respond to questions from people you meet. Look closely at the Republican Platform as it will have this issue expressed there.

Generally, the Republican party asks for lower taxes for all. They favor lower spending and a more cost-effective government. The Democrats will tell you they want more taxes and more spending. This alone should be a real help in winning over new voters ESPECIALLY if they are working. They know you cannot get something for nothing and the Democrats want to say the top 1% of taxpayers will pay for all the new spending. Just isn't going to happen. Simple policy discussion should suffice.

### 6. Healthcare
Obamacare was a major issue for years but now is pretty much in the background, but healthcare is not. We do not believe healthcare will be the make or break issue for 2020. We do believe it could have some meaningful impact and the issues could change quickly. STAY INFORMED. It seems as many as 80% of people with health insurance are satisfied.

### 7. Medicare and Social Security
These are issues extremely important to the elderly and persons about to retire. It is also important to candidates because these groups usually have one of the highest voter turnouts. The Democrats are actually weak on this issue because they are constantly trying to expand both programs with the concern that the expansion would introduce socialized medicine and some kind of socialized guaranteed assistance.

We again ask Patriots to step up and form again ad hoc committees and become absolutely knowledgeable on this issue. Then, compare facts with what the Democrats are pushing so as to mount a real campaign issue. The most obvious problem is if you add everyone, they will no longer be paid in programs. They will become government paid out programs. Many people as have paid for years into social security and medicare and look at the money having been paid into a trust with the government. People would be rightfully afraid that if non-payors were given benefits the people who paid would receive reduced benefits. There is also the notion of fairness. How fair is it to pay for something and then have your money taken to provide benefits for those who paid nothing.

## 8. Military Strength

The American public wants a strong military. They take pride in the power of the American armed forces. They provide security to our nation and to Americans abroad. A couple of issues might come up and we should be prepared to address them.

A federal district court ruled that an all-male universal draft is unconstitutional. With women now allowed to be in combat positions, there is no reason not to only require males to register for the draft. Does this mean the draft law will be ended by Congress repealing the law? We should start researching this issue so we are prepared and also know what the official position of the Republican National Committee as well as individual candidates on the issue.

It would be good to show how are military has performed and how President Trump has utilized forces to defeat ISIS. Stress how President Trump is forcing other nations to carry some of the financial load for world peace. Point out how he is bringing troops and other military home. Show how he wants to end over 50 years protecting a wall and border between North and South Korea. He also has a southern border to protect.

The military and many veterans are very pro Republican and very pro Donald Trump. They are aware that the President wants to "have their back" and wants the military to have the best of everything to defend our country.

### 9. Law and Order

With the Presidency of Obama, the debate on law and order has become a racial issue and an all-out attack against the professional law persons who provide law and order. President Trump has been a big supporter of law enforcement, first responders, firefighters and all who keep us safe.

This could become quite an issue but needs to be handled very factually and professionally. It starts by an in-depth research of the American attitude regarding police and law enforcement in general. Must distinguish between the Republicans Democrats. Other issues will dovetail into this one, such as "gun-control" and a comparison of places that have strict gun control and violence. The environment that has come when public figures and entertainers openly accuse police of racism and being killers. The effect of sanctuary cities and the obvious "nose-thumbing" of the law. The effect of illegal immigrants being harbored aided and abetted by various government entities and elected officials.

A collection of quotes from many left of center elected officials attacking police as the "bad guys" every time there was a shooting. Checkout the myriad of lawsuits against cities and others for false arrest and malicious prosecution of law enforcement. Call out the public figures who make accusations and when shown wrong, do not apologize, just go on to find someone else to attack

### 10. Drug addiction and homelessness

This is a two-part issue. Everyone, especially Democrats, are complaining we are not doing enough to stop the opioid crisis and the skyrocketing "overdose" deaths. Large part of it is tied to the issue of immigration. The majority of illicit drugs come to America by way of our Southern Border. Strengthening security there helps reduce the crisis. We need to incorporate this issue with immigration so that when we can maintain the initiative and keep the Democrats from taking two issues we embrace and turning them into theirs.

If this issue of drug addiction is extremely important to you, then follow up on President's statements about addressing the issue and YOU ADRESS THE ISSUE. Get together with some others so inclined and commence a podcast or a website that explains the President's sentiments and the multi-faceted approach to be taken to combat this situation. Let the people know that the best way to address the issue IS TO ELECT REPUBLICAN CANDIDATES and REELECT DONALD TRUMP.

### *11. Socialism or Capitalism and What Direction for America.*

Most of the Democrats having announced their run for president in 2020 are touting social and economic programs that are socialist. Some candidates even come right out and say so. They consider capitalism as the enemy. The most recent surveys show Americans prefer capitalism. The good reason why may be experience in the western hemisphere. All we need do is point to two socialist countries that were destroyed by socialism: Cuba under the Castro brothers and Venezuela under Maduro. If you hear people spouting the left-wing redistribution of wealth, just ask them to explain its continuing failures and point to Cuba and Venezuela.

These are not all the issues that may come to be addressed during the campaign. Stay alert to the news and the current political battles over issues. The more informed you are the more you can relay timely and accurate information to prospective voters.

The issues and how they are addressed may well determine the outcome of the election. You should obtain a copy of the platform of the Republican National Committee and any platforms of the candidates who will be on your ballot. To address issues you must be knowledgeable about the issues and the positions taken by variious parties. You should also obtain copies of the platforms of the Democrat party and their candidates so you know what your opposition is thinking and planning.

We believe our candidates and the Republican party are stronger on the issues. The positions taken are more inline with the majority of Americans.

The Democrats appear to be "preaching to the choir" in an "echo chamber." They are simply out of touch with vast American majority. You can tell when they start to publicly attack people who disagree with their positions as "stupid", "uneducated", "Christian fanatics", on and on.

The only element missing is our approach in getting the message out about our position on the issues. Make it a priority to let people know about our positions and platforms. We do this by countering any news media or political ad that distorts or attacks our positions. We make sure we always have copies of our platforms and issues to pass out to people we meet. Do not let a chance on social media or responding to news comments on various websites to wax eloquent on the issues.

The Red Wave taskforce "owns the issues" because we know the issues and the platforms and we know they are superior to the Democrats.

# CHAPTER 9

# KNOW ALL YOUR ENEMIES

In this 2020 campaign, the Democrat candidates, and the Democrat Party are not your only enemies. As was evident from the 2016 and 2018 campaigns there were two major institutions working hard to undermine the Republican candidates and made efforts to overturn the result of the presidential campaign. The two major players were first, the vast majority of the large news services and news networks. The other was most of the Federal government bureaucracy. There were other individuals and groups and we will discuss them, but the two just mentioned need to be addressed and essentially nullified or blunted.

Major complaint from last two elections was the amount of fake news and false stories. We need to capture the narrative by avoiding this ourselves. "… the truth will set you free." (John 8:32) Not many in the media and certainly not in the Democrat Party abide by this saying. It could be they seem to attack Christianity and the saying is mundane. Say anything and get elected. If we follow that approach, we will lose. SET THE NARRATIVE and gain the public trust by always sticking to the facts and truths. The following are black letter rules, as it is imperative that we always have the moral high ground and we are never on defense.

**Never knowingly make a false statement of fact;**

**Never assert a fact or story that you have not thoroughly researched and checked with multiple sources;**

**Never tell half-truths and embellish or exaggerate any story; Do not publish derogatory story or fact that has nothing directly to do with campaign;**

**Leave candidates children and family out of your publication unless it is important to the candidate and his campaign;**

**Do not participate in any subterfuge such as "false flag" representations or impersonating other candidates, parties or organizations.**

## *The Media Is Your Enemy*

The animus between President Trump and the main stream media is unparalleled in American history. The rhetoric of the reporters has actually turned the tide. In most instances, the American public believes main media has no credibility at all. Harvard and Harris did a poll for HillTV. What they found was 80% of Republicans believe the main stream media gives out "fake news." and 60% of independents feel that way. Even 53% of Democrats believe the mainstream media gives out fake news.

The question is why worry about the mainstream media? They are purveyors of "fake news." The previous poll also found that 84% of people found the news very confusing. They may think it is fake but which parts? They also do not know where else to get news of any kind. We need to end the dilemma. Provide social media and other networking to cover the most important stories of the day. Before there was any modern type communication such as telephones or radios, people somehow got the news. Granted, it could be rumors rather than totally accurate, but it did spread. We can also do the spreading if we all participate, BUT WE MUST VET OUR INFORMATION AS WELL. People will trust you as a news and information source if you always prove out as accurate. The most important job will be to challenge that which is fake so none rubs off on the voters. We have seen many of you already doing this but we need a concerted effort for this election cycle.

## *The "Deep State" is Your Enemy*

"The two enemies of the people are criminals and government..." Thomas Jefferson would not however believe what the government has been doing of late and especially in the Presidential election of 2016.

"When government fears the people, there is liberty. When the people fear the government, there is tyranny." Thomas Jefferson was making it very clear what he believed happens with the dynamics of government and the people it is supposed to serve. Ask yourself "Are people fearful of the government, such as IRS audits and administrative seizures without a court order?"

By now you have heard of the meetings between high level Department of Justice and FBI officials, plotting to remove or otherwise compromise the newly elected resident. The names of people who were at meeting s include James Comey, Former head of FBI; Rod Rosenstein, Deputy Attorney General; Andrew McCabe, deputy Direct of FBI; Peter Strzok, Senior FBI agent; Lisa Paige, FBI attorney and other ranking "deep State" connected to intelligence and law enforcement. They met according to admissions by some of the above-named individuals to find a way to get rid of President Trump. They discussed all types and methods. What is most distressing is this is not what America is about. The "deep state" works for us. We choose our elected officials, not them.

We also know that a special counsel was appointed to investigate an allegation of Russian collusion with the Trump campaign. We also know that the entire fiasco started with a bogus unverified dossier paid for the Democrats and hand delivered to the FBI. This whole process is so disgusting as it reeks of a third world back room coup attempt.

We do not have to just be disgusted. We are asking Patriots reading this book to take up the mission of doing an in-depth report on his entire episode so we can broadcast it to the public. However, since it is election year 2020, we will stress how the Democrats help launch this and how they colluded with the Deep State to highjack an election or to take down an elected president. This should be a high priority mission and should be a collective effort by groups. Let us know when you have a completed report. The intent is to make the Democrat collusion with deep state an issue for 2020.

## *Wealthy Elites Are Often Your Enemy*

By December 26, 2018 the news media was reporting an apology publicly made by Reid Hoffman, a co-founder of Linkedin, a business networking internet site. The apology was to the public and Roy Moore for funding a tech campaign with American Engagement Technologies in 2017 to oppose Roy Moore's campaign to be elected senator from Alabama. Mickey Dickerson, a former Obama admin official, misinformation campaign on Facebook and Twitter set up the program and it was a false misdirection social media blitz making it look like Russian persons were supporting Roy Moore.

Then there is billionaire Tom Steyer who set aside 10 million in 2017 to run ads for impeachment of Trump. He is also supporting any candidate who will promise to vote to impeach the president. We have not seen any high crimes and misdemeanors and Steyer is pushing obviously because he does not like Trump or his policy. However, Steyer is using his wealth to push a false narrative. His actions are not what we need in politics today. Legitimate differences on policy yes, but a negative campaign to charge someone with crimes and convict him after impeachment without sufficient grounds is unfair. In fact, he should be careful because lobbying and paying people to charge someone could be construed as unlawful. If he is insinuating that he will provide donations to congresspeople who in return vow to vote for impeachment, then he may have some problems

Do not be intimidated by the elitist wealthy liberals. They make mistakes and often their arrogance is their undoing. We cannot afford to have the election bought by money from Steyer and other elites.

## *The Entertainment Community Is Often Your Enemy*

The entertainment industry seems to have more people supporting liberal agendas and supporting the Democrats. These people are in public eye already and often given plenty of press on political issues and candidates. With the press often pro-liberal they will give entertainers an extraordinary amount of press coverage. We need to counter them and neutralize them. Let people know that just because they have star quality in show business does not mean they are knowledgeable about serious matters like politics foreign affairs, and national security.

We can point out the foolish waste of news time from uninformed entertainers. What we cannot do is disregard them. Even if they sound foolish, they will get their message out and there are some voters who might begin to believe some of what they say. Always challenge and counter any aggressive attack from a celebrity type.

### The Educational Community is Often Your Enemy

Most of us have seen those pictures of men dressed in women's clothing reading storybooks to 5 and 6 year old school children. Most have read articles about transgender boys competing in girl's track and field and wrestling and winning all the top prizes It should be obvious that there are entrenched members of the education field who have a social and political agenda. Ronald Reagan said we are just "…one generation away from socialism."

It gets more intense and worse at colleges around the country. Professors are allowed to call for violence and discrimination based on sex, race and religion as long as the person being singled out is white straight male and possibly a Christian. We have seen violence directed at conservative students and out and out harassment go unchecked. Free speech is dead on many campuses. In both high school and college you might receive retaliation from professors or teachers if you do not follow the liberal political line. It is estimated almost 80% of faculty at college level are liberal. They often ridicule students who are not liberal as they are. They can retaliate on grades. It can be very scary.

There are some college organizations formed to combat this wasteland in Highschool and college, but it is tough going. Fight back.

Start with vouchers. You cannot brainwash little children if they are not forced to attend a mind control school. It is the biggest weapon at primary grades. Run for school district board of trustees. Point out the terrible policies and activities at your schools. Stage protests. (peaceable of course) Start a Parent Concerned National group to explore the decay in education and the proselytizing of children and all students by the faculty and others.

Education is a very hot issue with many parents and it needs to be exposed and challenged.

### *Target Mission Force*

Many of you have made comments on interactive news online, social media and other outlets your absolute displeasure with certain long time Democratic leaders. Now you can spearhead the charge to remove them and address other serious issues.

We want the Taskforce to join in TMF where we target individuals, issues and institutions that have a major impact on the 2020 election. As always, we do not condone or allow false or fraudulent stories and publications. There is plenty of real factual data to support the targeting. The following are examples, Individuals: Hillary Clinton, as she remains active in the news media and many Democrats take boldness from her ability to be invincible despite conduct that would surely have seen criminal charges for another person. Targeting should be a constant campaign duration project with all Task Force members contributing. Special care to stay on top of all media and news releases concerning Hillary and work up of responses. Tactics should be those discussed in Chapter Four. Issues: 84 per cent of Americans are against late term abortions in polls taken after New York legislature passed law allowing abortions after the twentieth month and apparently all the way to a partial birth abortion. Do stay on top of this issue and do get the word out. Make the Democrats own this policy or denounce it. Either way it is a hard-hitting issue in the campaign.

Institutions: DNC. Let us see if the Democratic Committee does an encore of last presidential election in which the Party leaders took a partisan position and literally did everything they could to prevent Bernie Sanders from getting the nomination in 2016. We do want you to keep a close watch on this institution, as they give us substance to call out their political shortcomings and also to keep alerted as to any attacks or claims they are making against our candidates and our platform. The plan is to stay observant and stay connected in enlightening others in the Taskforce of what you have learned.

### *Must be Ready to Counter and Neutralize the Enemies.*

When you find the enemy (they are really everywhere and most will let you know loud and clear who they are), study and research them to see if they are vulnerable or their arguments are vulnerable. AGAIN, research and observance and no fantasy claims PLEASE. We have seen many of you on Facebook and other social media uploading videos and charts showing you did heavy research to debunk an enemy's public attacks or allegations. We ask you to keep that up but channel it, not just to your social site, but to all Taskforce people and ask them to repost or share and make it a deluge. Do not stop there. You should have elected officials on "speed dial" so they always get a copy. Yes, send a copy to the offending enemy. No unsubstantiated attacks or fake attacks by the enemies will go unchallenged.

# CONCLUSION

There was a time when young children walked to school without fear of harm. Their schools had no armed police. There was a time when we went to an airport and did not have to pass through metal detectors. Many of you will look around and see a nation in decline, a culture overtaken by a counterculture of excesses and evil. How did this happen?

There were those who gave accurate predictions of the coming changes in America. Aldous Huxley in his book *Brave New World* which was published in 1932 predicted political correctness, end of family based social units, oral contraception, and free sex, free drugs, and free feely videos. The book has always been considered a futuristic science fiction. Now it is seen as more prophetic look at America. The other science fiction writer, but later considered prophetic, was George Orwell who wrote *1984.* Orwell portrayed a totalitarian society based on hate and fear and government spying. He included televisions in homes that could spy on the average citizen and provide propaganda in its broadcasts.

There were many who quite early however, that foresaw the slippery slope of a decadent socialist type society. In 1965 a popular radio commentator named Paul Harvey made a radio broadcast that was disturbing but not wholly believed. He titled his broadcast as *"IF I WERE THE DEVIL."* He described what he foresaw as a society starting to slip into decadence and immoral conduct sapping the character of our society. In 1996 Mr. Harvey did a video recording of the same speech but updated to include chronicled activity since his early speech by the same name. It is this one that people should read or watch as it has been placed on You Tube. You can find the speeches by typing in any search engine the name Paul Harvey and the title.

The question remains: how, did we get from 1965 to 1996 to the present with an obvious slip into a moral decay in America?

*" Evil flourishes when good men do nothing"…(attributed to Edmund Burke.)* It was not that good men did nothing, it was the way evil was introduced into our society. The drug dealer does not try to recruit drug users from independent adults. No, he recruits children and teenagers. He knows they will grow up drug users and that generation will be more tolerant of drug use and set an environment of extensive drug use for the following generation. The ultra-liberals, the left socialists, the social ultra-progressives have followed the same path. They have targeted school children and teens to recruit their social ideology. They have infiltrated out schools at every level and they can be found in the news industry and the entertainment industry. Worst of all they have been embraced by the Democrat party and their candidates.

Then, there was the general election of 2016. An outsider ran for President on a platform of essentially returning America to its roots and apply the principles and character of the "Greatest Generation." He was elected and brought the slide of our country into a counterculture to a halt. His election was just the beginning as the bigger battle is coming in 2020.

We are excited to get the Taskforce up and going. Our plan is to schedule workshops, seminars, and rallies where we can meet others, share ideas and information. Look for coming events on our website, as well as, follow us on social media. Check out www.Redwavetaskforce.com often and keep up to date. We welcome your ideas for our website and upcoming events.

# CHECK US OUT

Redwavetaskforce.com
Redwavetaskforce@gmail.com

Thank you for reading this book. Only a dedicated Patriot would take the time and attention to read the book. It is not the end, but the beginning. Join us in a grass roots movement to bring a Red Wave Victory in November 2020. Accept our invitation to be a part of the Red Wave Taskforce. It is responsible people like yourself, this country needs to show the way. Welcome aboard.

# APPENDIX A
# PERSONAL INVENTORY

Name ______________________________________________

| *Office* | *Name* | *(X) Up for Election* |
|---|---|---|
| President | Donald Trump | X |
| U.S. Senator | | |
| US Congressman | | |
| Governor | | |
| State Senator | | |
| State Representative | | |
| Other State Officers | | |
| Local Officers | | |
| Other Candidates | | |

# APPENDIX B

# REPUBLICAN PARTY CONTACTS

Republican National Committee   www.gop.com

Ronna McDaniel, Chairwoman
Telephone: 202-863-8500
310 First Street, SE
Washington, DC 20003

State of _________________________________________ Republican Party

Address _____________________________________________________

Email or website ______________________________________________

Telephone Number _____________________________________________

County of _________________________________ Republican Committee

# APPENDIX C

# FILE FOLDER FOR ALL TASKFORCE

The following is a list of documents you should have in a file folder which you take with you everywhere. Use this as a checklist.

1.  Copy of this book.
2.  Personal survey inventory.
3.  Republican Party contacts sheet'
4.  Candidate contact sheet.
5.  Copy of chart comparing Republican and Democrat parties historically.
6.  Copy of latest Success of President Trumps administration.
7.  Spiral notebook.
8.  Campaign materials for each candidate in your voting area.

# APPENDIX D

## Saul Alinsky's 13 Rules for Radicals

(excerpted from Saul Alinsky's Book: *Rules for Radicals*, published in 1971)

1. "Power is not what you have, but what the enemy thinks you have."
2. "Never go outside the expertise of your people."
3. "Whenever possible go outside the expertise of the enemy."
4. "Make the enemy live up to its own book of rules. "
5. "Ridicule is man's most potent weapon."
6. "A good tactic is one your people enjoy."
7. "A tactic that drags on too long becomes a drag."
8. "Keep the pressure on, never let up."
9. "The threat is usually more terrifying than the thing itself."
10. "The major premise for tactics is the development of operations that will maintain constant pressure upon the opposition."
11. "If you push a negative hard enough, it will push through and become a positive."
12. "The price of a successful attack is a constructive alternative."
13. "Pick the target, freeze it, personalize it, and polarize it.

### Saul Alinsky's 11 Rules on the Ethics of Means and Ends.

1. "One's concern with the ethics of means and ends varies inversely with one's personal issue in the issue."
2. "The judgment of the ethics of means is dependent upon the political position of those sitting in judgment."
3. "In war the ends justify almost any means."
4. "Judgment must be made in context of there times in which the action occurred and not from other chronological vantage points."
5. "Concern with ethics increases with the number of means available and vice versa."
6. "The less important end to be desired, the more one can afford to

engage in ethics evaluations of means."

7. "Generally, success or failure is a might determinant of ethics." "Morality of means depends upon whether the means is being employed at a time of imminent defeat or imminent victory."

8. "Any effective means is automatically judged by the opposition as being unethical."

9. "You do what you can with what you have and clothe it in moral garments."

10. "Goals must be phrased in general terms like 'Liberty, Equality, Fraternity,' 'Of the common welfare,' 'Pursuit of Happiness,' or 'Bread

# Resources on Campaign and Election Laws

General Background on the reporting and regulating election laws:

www.Wikipedia.com
www.Ballotpedia.org
www.usa.gov/voting laws
www.fec.gov/help-candidates and committees
www.fec.gov/resources/cms-content/documents/fecapdf
www.NCSL.org/research/elections

Check out the League of Women Voter's website. It is helpful in assisting Recruiting as it provides specific information on how to register to vote for each Individual:

www.vote411.org/voterguide

# APPENDIX F

# Most Popular Political Websites

www.Huffingtonpost.com www.Breitbart.com www.Politico.com
www.Slate.com www. Breitbart.com  www.Politico.com  www.Slate.com
www.Dailycaller.com www.dailykos.com  www.Infowars.com
www.SALON.om www.TheBlaze.com www. WND.com
www.NEWSMAX.com www.Washingtontimes.com
www.MotherJones.com


**WATCHDOG WEBSITES FOR GOVERNMENT AND POLITICS**
www.Judicialwatch.com
www.Openthebooks.com
www.factdc.org


**Taxes**
www.cagw.org
www.caltax.org

# NOTICE

This book is meant to be educational material. The writings are the opinions, suggestions, recommendations of the author. Readers should consult their own attorney, accountant or other experts to address issues or questions personal to them. The author has suggested throughout the book that readers consult with other experts and knowledgeable people for advice.

The readers should do their own due diligence as well when reading this book by researching and verifying for themselves matters discussed in the book.

This book is not endorsed or approved or authorized by any other individual or Organization.

9 781977 209856